wild like a woman

poems by

Thalia Geiger

Finishing Line Press
Georgetown, Kentucky

wild like a woman

Copyright © 2025 by Thalia Geiger
ISBN 979-8-88838-971-3 First Edition
All rights reserved under International and Pan-American Copyright Conventions.
No part of this book may be reproduced in any manner whatsoever without written
permission from the publisher, except in the case of brief quotations embodied in
critical articles and reviews.

ACKNOWLEDGMENTS

Big thanks to the following publications who saw promise in these poems,
and thus saw promise in me:

Black Fox Literary Review—"Lavender & Damiana"
The Paddock Review—"Soft Against the Stone"
Frontier Poetry—"pitiful, adj."

Publisher: Leah Huete de Maines
Editor: Christen Kincaid
Cover Art: Leroy Geiger
Author Photo: Tammi Geiger
Cover Design: Elizabeth Maines McCleavy

Order online: www.finishinglinepress.com
also available on amazon.com

Author inquiries and mail orders:
Finishing Line Press
PO Box 1626
Georgetown, Kentucky 40324
USA

Contents

"*There is a time in our lives, usually mid-life, when a woman has to make a decision—possibly the most important psychic decision of her future life—and that is, whether to be bitter or not.*"

—Clarissa Pinkola Estés, *Women Who Run With the Wolves*

GOING OFF MY MEDS AGAIN

I'm going off my meds again
while the world around

is catching on fire, orange skies
and fully bloomed flowers

popping fuchsia into the eye-line.
It's Beltane so every candle

I could find is lit in my home.
People practice rituals

for fertility today and every day
for the rest of the summer.

I make no plans to abandon
my birth control, my partner

not finding fondness
in the idea of a babe.

As a woman, there wasn't always,
but there is an ember now

glowing within, wanting
to make and be made.

I hear it singing in the dark.
Like the sound of individual waves

cresting then sloshing on sand,
letting you know there

is a whole ocean behind it.
It acts of its own volition

the way all flora and fauna do.
We season our bodies

every year for this great grinding
of mortar to pestle. We make

substance from nothing else.
I too live in a grind,

for nothing to come of it,
but a building of a garden

no one tends to.

LAVENDER & DAMIANA

I'm at that point where I have
to straddle you to look into your eyes
and nothing comes of it but staring.

The world slides sideways,
sinking laterally, meaning my medication
has taken its hold

so I'm doing everything I can
to be sexy and squeeze the essence
out of greyed lavender buds

and damiana leaves. Here we are
in the bedroom, new, and not knowing
enough despite all our trying.

You sit dissatisfied and upright against
the headboard, sucking down
cigarettes made of clove

to lessen the addictions and manage
your mistakes by getting ash
all over the new bedspread.

Past the poplars outside, people dig
through humble dirt and scavenge
for their lives, letting their loved ones'

desires swallow them whole.
I'd love to meet your soul
but I haven't met mine yet.

That's the only truth we know.

MOTHERING

I want to talk about mothering
without the mention of a child.

I am a childless mother every day,
sidestepping ants on the sidewalk.

I join in on a trine of cracked voices
howling along in a bar to a pop song

as if it is the only moon. I casually wipe
crusted fluid out the corner of my cat's eyes

with my bare finger. Even he knows
I am his mother, tilts his tiny animal chin

up to let me. I am mother to every bug
I've escorted out of my house

with caution, instead of killed. A mother
in the care taken to fill glass jars

with rainwater to re-soak
the sun-scorched greenery outside.

I am mother to the air to listen to the wind
before a thunderstorm, how it complains

and begs my forgiveness before it wrecks
my patio, overturning all my potted plants.

The dirt spills out onto the inlaid stones
I rescue like a mother with a gentle touch

from each crevice so as not to crumble
it further and replace it where it once was.

Yes, everywhere, it all exists at once:
I see every woman as my mother

and yet I carry the whole world
in my womb.

SOFT AGAINST THE STONE

She is sitting on a rock like some goddess,
foot curled up in comfortability.
Her softness against the stone like gray
morning light against deep, red earth.
She doesn't wonder. What's right
in front of her tells her everything
she needs to know. Her brow is cool,
relaxed. Eyes trained ahead and only
ahead at the world. She is steady
and sure, just as the mountains
know substantial winds but withstand
them. Just as the crocuses in this white
spring open their mouths at every
afternoon's warmth like clockwork,
knowing what they know.

TO-DO LIST
after Ama Codjoe

Gonna lay down my razor.
Gonna slip into my winter body and plough the earth
    with my every roll.
Gonna step on all these toes.
Gonna reach out my hand and touch, touch, touch
    every petal I meet, every shaking leaf.
Gonna write my own music with the doves every
    morning until I understand the weight of my own
    voice.
Gonna watch their soft-chested feathers ruffle
    in the wind as they listen.
Gonna lay down in god's green field and pick the tiny
    golden flowers with my teeth.
Gonna infect the world with my bleeding.
Gonna wander into the dark and find my home there.
Gonna eat. A lot.
Gonna let the juices stain my teeth and paint my chin
    like an Inuit's tattoo.
Gonna wear my pearls and know I've earned them.
Gonna run, pounding heels and heartbeats. For once,
    not in fear of anything, but as a way to regulate
    my ever-quaking breath. Gonna run as a way
    to prepare myself for infinite flight.

LITANY OF EVERYTHING WOMAN

The pink hollyhocks in the garden.
The smell and shape of radishes.
Candle melts.
Homemade root beer.
Thunder during a snowstorm.
The color of dawn rising
above mountains.
Summer rains.
The smooth texture and flavor
of caramel.
Any shade of red,
especially auburn,
or burgundy.
Every inch of invasive ivy.
Ponds.
Plums.
Basil.
Salt in ice cream.
Crows, calling in the distance.
Moss-covered forests in bloom.
Dew on spider webs.
Knowing the words but still
humming along to a song.
Sugar sweet.
Bitter coffee.
The whole river,
and everything that lives
inside it.

BRALESS IN SPRING

don't say it's wrong
to want nothing more
than to be braless in the spring
and singing some melody
that bounces off the surface
of the jade green lake I'm in
the sun dipping in and out
the world unfocused because
I've left my glasses back
at shore

how bad is it
if I just make my life like this
leave my brain back home
adopt the mentality
of a siren not so shyly
twirling my hair to show
that there is nothing
above this pleasure
to touch and be
touched?

WOMAN AS WITCHERY

like semi-precious gemstones
each with their own hardness
like garnet thick and clotted
like blood often made of iron
and blowing around smoke

like incense and ash
as powder and shadow
bending slender as rings
of salt circling everything

like a peacock's feather
floating in the air
with its watchful eye
surrounded by a thousand
barbs with a thousand
silken hands to touch

like hagstones with holes
the art of seeing
through the wound
the womb

like wormwood
like cornflower and chamomile
satchels stitched up
with mugwort
with motherwort
like lilacs and clove.

everywhere we go,
the moon follows.

WILD LIKE A WOMAN & WET LIKE A CHILD

If there is no mother, she learns the way to shave her legs from the other girls in her class. She learns the way the prickled hair grows fast and easy, the way the weeds poke through concrete on the street. This early, she learns she is like the earth but knows nothing of it yet. She wields a razor either too sharp or blunt-edged and slides a path through the trees. If she did it right, she sees her body barren, bald and hairless. Everything properly preened, she'll get up dizzy from the tub and sit frozen in her towel until the sensation that's settled disappears: a cross between feeling wild like a woman, and wet like a child.

UNANSWERABLE

can you please speak up don't you want me to help you have you tried asking them nicely do you really not know how to sew who taught you how to do that why don't you put your hair up today is that the only thing you know how to cook do you own a slip dress and you paid how much for that do you really want that life for yourself why won't you color your hair how about you just come over are you alone why were you alone why don't you sit straight why don't you just really another one don't you want kids are you sure you don't want another one don't you want them to like you don't you do you really want that life for yourself and what about marriage and that's what you're wearing and you did what are you even wearing a bra don't you shave are you really gonna do that are you sure about that you really think you can handle that oh all by yourself how about you calm yourself don't you want to know these things so you don't make a fool of yourself do you really want that life for yourself do you really want this life for yourself?

FORGIVE MYSELF

I try to forgive myself today
for letting the tea go cold.
For eating nothing but navel oranges
well into the late afternoon.
Am I living incorrectly?
To the women who always right
the wrongs and keep the kettle on,
do what you do. We're all
waiting on the world to change
in our own ways. I'll do what I do.
All day through the windows
I watch curling leaves
bend to the wind's rhythm.
With people I make a mess
of things. I'm gullible. I fall in love.
I leave them. I owe the poet
Linda Gregg my life.
And still, I stay secluded
all the while in this damp house
full of maroon light and linens,
loving the downpour outside
with the way it keeps me in.

EARTH FROM HEAVEN

I couldn't do this again,
being trapped in heaven.

Louise Glück said it first:
from up here, the earth glitters
like the moon.

Let me just admire that.

When you grieve, it's monsoon
season. I have smaller griefs
I grieve quietly and often.

Up here I see guava trees
and even though the warm
breezes blow and the red sun
shines, there is nothing
touching me.

In my tears are every earthly moment
of tragedy, can't you see them?

Don't you want to lick them off
my swollen cheeks?

Or are you too,
afraid to touch me?

PORTRAIT OF A WOMAN

It's always that depiction of her,
like Lady Godiva on a horse,
strong and white-bodied, copper
hair down her back like a red river,
running and kicking up flecks
of earth on a black-sanded beach
behind her. Instead of a woman,
just a woman, not even sitting
in a light-filled meadow but just
on her cluttered porch steps,
the concrete below biting
into her jean shorts, staring down
at the red wine stains on her
lily-white shoes. She's not thinking
of anything more special
than the fact that she'll never
manage to get the stains out,
but that's okay because the shoes
aren't really ugly, just a little pink
now, starting their second life.

SELF-CARE

Is it a softening or a sharpening
when we file our everything
with pumice stones?

We are rage and rhythm
all in the same breath,
and they fear both.

PITIFUL, ADJ.

After Alison C. Rollins

a. evoking or deserving of pity. b. shameful and deserving of spit. c. as in, "isn't she just"; d. as in, "you must not be talking about *me*". e. the lot we got. f. often a noose we tie around our swan-like necks. g. as in: too slender, too much, too little, too late. h. seen in: being excited that lyft has a new feature to pair you with another woman driver. i. usually the thing in its entirety. j. example: me. k. example: probably you, too.

SCREAMING

Give me something with teeth,
I need to battle against something
other than myself. I want the feel
of fire and lashings, not this
awkward begging to be undone.

The humidity continues to swell
this time of year.
The Women's March newsletter
sends me cryptic subjects:
nobody is coming to save us.
Everyday there are still women
disappearing and I want
to become one.

I want to walk outside
to try it but there's a cicada
stuck in my storm door,
the big green-beige body
wedged between glass
and swirling iron.
My whole body shudders
at the sight of its legs curled
up in prayer or comfort.
I wonder where its family
is, if it even has one.

We come to know ourselves
when we have nothing,
when all the doors of the world
slam shut in our faces.
I've tasted wood in my mouth
and countless times still
wake up with the splinters
wet on my tongue.

Today, every day,
and every hour, I decide against
walking into an onslaught
of traffic. It is my way
of keeping time.
And every time I want
to leave my house, like a bell,
I think of the cicada's
defiant body still there
fastened against the entrance
to my world, half-alive
and screaming, screaming.

WOMAN IS LITANY

I see the twisted faces of women
like ancient gnarled trees

and know I am with them
when I hear the news

of the government trying
again to take away someone's

rights. This time our wombs
are rentable space.

In this female climate
every day is a rainstorm

of rocks against
the tenderest of skin

and I can see that to be
a woman is to be a litany,

starting with god
as an exasperation

because my birth control
causes my gut problem,

my flora, my microbiome,
my arms flailing over sheets

and awkward knees
on the ground digging

under my bed looking
for that tiny yellow

pill I dropped and lost
somewhere in the carpet fibers.

My lost earring backing
I found but not

my only route for control.
Oh, my silly hands.

Oh, stress. Oh, media.
Oh, microbikini.

Oh, every anxiety.
My baseline,

my through line,
my trauma, my rotting,

my discarded fruit
on marble countertops,

my ability and inability
to abandon my body

in bed, in beds,
my slithering, my sinking,

my sex.
I lost it just

as quickly as it takes
a man to tug again

at your bra strap
after you've just

told him no. I've read
so many poems

about motherhood
and still don't know

if I'll ever want
to be one. Here this

is supposed to be
another poem about me

or women and yet
it is another poem

about men.

SEPTEMBER IN THE PARK

I happen to look over my shoulder
and find a child who was staring
at me all along, round-faced
and happily curious.

Her mother calls
to her from across the green
lawn and so the child runs
into her arms, where the mother
lifts her skyward.
The child kicks her feet,
knowing she's safe
even in this weightlessness.

Though the end of summer
has yielded so much rain,
the air now is cool with certainty.
I can see every soft blade
of grass and all this openness
makes me wonder if this
world is for me,
and if I even want it.

TO GIRLHOOD, FROM WOMANHOOD

You may not learn to love me yet.
I will forgive that for you.

It's not so much a currency as you think,
forgiveness—but something to pass along
to the next person like the eldest sister's
woven sweater or a sweet scent on the wind.

Dawn is coming in on the horizon,
showing you all the colors
you can paint yourself with.

Sun yourself before
the cold comes, for me.

You can rest here as often as you'd like.
And even when your voice is gone,
and you call out to me
in your gray, mute whisper,

I will hear you through the blackest
midnights, and through the blankest dark.

I will always hear you.

GIRLHOOD|WOMANHOOD II

yet you think
along woven winds

the horizon paints
with your colors

but it's me coming
it's me looking

after you
like a silent call

you whisper
and time whispers

back to you

Thalia Geiger is a writer from Philadelphia, Pennsylvania. She holds a BFA in Creative Writing from The University of the Arts. After studying both poetry and fiction, she embarked on a career in literary publishing. She placed as a finalist in *Atlanta Review*'s 2020 International Poetry Contest Issue, and her poetry has appeared in *New York Quarterly, Allegory Ridge, Santa Ana River Review, and more. Her fiction has appeared in Coffin Bell and Grim & Gilded.* She currently works as a publishing associate and poetry editor. You can catch up with her on her Instagram, @thalierr or on her website, *thaliageiger.com.*

www.ingramcontent.com/pod-product-compliance
Lightning Source LLC
Chambersburg PA
CBHW022100080426
42734CB00009B/1437